THE STOOP

poems by

Jeff Saperstein

Finishing Line Press
Georgetown, Kentucky

THE STOOP

Copyright © 2021 by Jeff Saperstein
ISBN 978-1-64662-428-7 First Edition
All rights reserved under International and Pan-American Copyright Conventions. No part of this book may be reproduced in any manner whatsoever without written permission from the publisher, except in the case of brief quotations embodied in critical articles and reviews.

ACKNOWLEDGMENTS

Versions of several of the poems in this collection first appeared in the following journals:

Aries, "Swing"
Lone Stars, "Turkish Bath," "Between Two Houses"
Darkling Magazine, "Alley Cats"
The Deronda Review, "Where Were You When"
Stickman Review, "Uncle Nachman's Numbers," "Their Knowledge," "Infinitive"
Common Ground Review, "The Minimalist," "Objects in Mirror"
Chantarelle's Notebook, "Quasi-," "Hitchcock the Boy," "Crossword," "In the Event That…"
Abbey, "Summer Interior"
Main Street Rag, "Melville's Second Son"
The Sow's Ear, "The Immigrants"
Ibbetson Street Press, "Forecast"
Westward Quarterly, "White Out"
Floyd County Moonshine, "A King of Tweets and Twitters"

Many thanks to the following people for their advice and support: Chelsea Adams, Justin Askins, Carolyn Mathews, Tim Poland, Steve Sternbach, and Linda Waggaman.

Publisher: Leah Huete de Maines
Editor: Christen Kincaid
Cover Art: Susan De Vries
Author Photo: Lisa Saperstein
Cover Design: Elizabeth Maines McCleavy

Order online: www.finishinglinepress.com
also available on amazon.com

Author inquiries and mail orders:
Finishing Line Press
PO Box 1626
Georgetown, Kentucky 40324
USA

Table of Contents

The Stoop 1
Swing 2
Turkish Bath 3
Alley Cats 4
Matinee 5
5th Grade 6
Where Were You When…? 7
Uncle Nachman's Numbers 8
The Minimalist 9
Their Knowledge 10
Shylock in Church 11
Quasi- 12
Hitchcock the Boy 13
Chiller Theatre: The Bride 14
Summer Interior 15
Melville's Second Son 16
Forecast 17
Crossword 18
The Immigrants 19
Between Two Houses 20
White Out 21
Infinitive 22
Objects in Mirror 23
In the event that… 24
A King of Tweets and Twitters 25
So Many Things 26
The Recliner 27
Introduction to Italian 28
Baffled 29
In My Dotage 30

For Lisa, naturally

The Stoop

Its pebbled brick bit into your thighs
when you sat on the top step
that in-between hour before supper.
The chrome-plated Avenue R bus
ground back and forth,
its exhaust mixing with a salt breeze
coming down Ocean Ave.

It was a corner stoop
so they came from all directions,
humankind parading before your elevated perch—
      Yeshiva boys in their long overcoats
      Catholic girls in plaid skirts
      double-breasted suits followed by Henry,
      the super, in overalls, walking his surly mutt.

Whether striding or ambling,
they would not acknowledge you,
never looked up. And you came to accept
your anonymity, saw the virtue
of the impersonal.
This is where you first learned
how to detach, the fine art
of taking it all in—
      the coarse and the smooth
      the sleek and the dull
with perfect equanimity.

Swing

"Higher, higher,"
we squealed to our fathers,
returning to the earth,
knowing our little legs
couldn't pump us to the sky.

Our fathers would always oblige.

We could feel the pressure
of their strong hands on our backs
as they launched us feet over head.
Soaring high above the playground fence,
we held tight to the cold metal chains,
knowing it was not impossible
we would die.

Turkish Bath

When I was seven,
my grandfather took me to Surf Avenue,
to the Turkish Bath.
I seemed to be the only child
amid the fog and tile and slippery passageways,
in this swamp of old men,
towels around their vast waists.

On Surf Avenue
I passed through a turnstile,
unclothing at the locker,
then stole down the steps
of the octagonal schvitz bath.
Five fleshy men sat in the mist,
their hairy arms resting on the ledge.
They smelled of Mennen and sour pickles
and they spoke of the ponies, pinochle,
and the Bums.
I did not like to think about
what hung below them, hidden
under the murky water.

When we left Surf Avenue, Poppy asked,
"So vot you tink, sonny boy,
you vant to coom mit me next veek?
The bets are goot for pores, goot for sinuses."
"No thanks," I mumbled,
my skin still moist with sweat.

Alley Cats

Armed with slingshots,
we stalked alley cats after school,
and once I hit a scrawny tabby with a stone.
It let out an unearthly yowl, fangs ivory,
pink tongue curled out full,
blood dripping from an eye.
Some primal instinct urged us
to prey on these ugly creatures.
Alley cats were freaks
like the unshaven super in greasy overalls
who crept down his narrow alley
into the boiler room, where he slept—
surely a place of demons.
A refugee, he spoke in a clotted tongue—
Hungarian, our parents said—
saliva spritzing from his canines
when he cursed us for pitching pennies
against the stucco wall. We named him
"the Ghoulash," and gave him the finger
when we sped past on our bikes.
Armed with ignorance and stones,
we took aim at all strangers
who trespassed on our turf.

Matinee

Your greatest fear was quicksand,
that illusion of solid ground.
At the Avalon, just two blocks from home,
you saw a man swallowed whole,
so slowly sucked in by the glop
it took several minutes of screen time
before he was gone from the frame.
In each next shot,
there was less of him to see.

First it took him below the knees,
left him more or less intact.
But as he strained against the suction,
the camera came in close cutting off
his legs. A bug-eyed torso,
he seemed no longer human.
When the muck was at his chin,
he let loose an effeminate shriek
like Fay Wray in the palm of the beast.
Then he went down.
For a long minute, the camera held
on the placid surface of the swamp.

When you came back up
into the sunlit world of Kings Highway,
your eyes squinted tight and your legs wobbled
on the paved street.

5th Grade

In 4th grade,
I pulled a chair back
and a chubby girl, Sarah,
fell hard on the linoleum floor,
her pink panties on display.
My parents were called
to Mrs. Gordon's office
three times after school.
All year my penmanship
was marked "unsatisfactory."

In 6th grade,
I had a crush on the new girl, Ronnie;
I cried out her name all night
in Frankie Valli's piercing falsetto.
On student talent night,
I recited, by heart, the names of the 33 Presidents,
from Washington to JFK;
Mrs. Glass smiled her praise.

I don't remember a thing
about 5th grade—
not the teacher's name,
or the boy or girl
I shared a desk with,
not the artwork or the posters
in homage to a forgotten theme,
not even the location of the closets
where we kept our outworn coats.

Where were you when . . . ?

Eighth grade homeroom:
day-dreamin' out the window;
an hour of good daylight left,
plenty of time for a game of 3 on 3.
Enter Mrs. Rudd, hands cupping her face...

> [We had played at assassination that fall,
> "Julius Caesar," Mrs. Rudd's favorite play.
> We had rehearsed the scene again and again
> but in the auditorium on opening night
> we hesitated— eight gawky boys in bed sheets,
> pinned very securely in back.
> Suddenly Gary Levine shouted
> to his parents in the last row,
> "Speak hands for me!"
> That was our cue:
> with cardboard, tin-foiled daggers
> we slaughtered Lawrence Cohen.
> After a suitable pause,
> Lawrence rose from the dead to recite
> "Friends, Romans, Countrymen,"
> eulogizing himself to enthusiastic applause].

. . .Enter Mrs. Rudd, bouffant hair out of place,
trembling, unable to deliver her speech,
shaken by an emotion we had never seen.
And this, just this, is the thing that stays:
not the dead President
or even Oswald getting it on tv—
but the tyrant teacher cut down, in tears,
a mere messenger speeding to the scene.
We lent her our ears.

Uncle Nachman's Numbers

When he rolled up his sleeves
to fry the potatoes in the sizzling oil,
I glimpsed them on his forearm—
6 digits etched in a sick blue ink.
I saw them and did not ask
what they added up to.
A 12-year old boy knows nothing
of the past. The latkes sizzled in the pan
and took form.

Back then, everyone cooked with gas
so he'd crisp them just right.
I tried to focus on the beads of oil
popping in the pan and the pale mix
turning gold, but my eyes kept drifting
to the numbers,
engraved on his arm for life.

A few knickknacks were scattered about
but he kept no photo of his wife and child
anywhere that I could see.
He'd fry dozens of pancakes,
latkes all day long.
The apartment filled with acrid smoke,
and the numbers gave off a palpable heat.

The Minimalist

On the blank leaves
of my father's "Abridged Prayer Book
For Jews in the Armed Forces,"
he kept a record in a green-blue ink
that hasn't faded much since '45.
I often glance at it, half expecting
the revelation that doesn't come.
The first entry, exactly as it reads:
12/5/42—Inducted at 5 Regt. Armory Balto, Md.

He uses a clipped style throughout the text,
each item beginning with a crisp verb
that marches down the page:
      Left
      Arrived
      Boarded
      Landed.
I keep waiting for an exclamation, an opinion,
a point of view, but all he offers me
are these abbreviated facts. When he notes
2/28/44—Arrived on Anzio Beach Head (8:00 am)
I'm forced to imagine his fears by the things
he doesn't say. He stubbornly omits
all personal pronouns, as if a camera's eye records
10/1/44—Wounded by shrapnel in Grenoble, France in 3 places.
Eleven entries mark his surgeries and hospital stays;
not once does he register a syllable of pain.
Then he's back on the stage,
rejoining his company, entering Germany, crossing the Rhine.
The pace is breath-taking, his restraint
maddening. He merely jots
5/4/45—Entered Dachau
as if there were nothing more
one could possibly say.

Their Knowledge
    (based on a photo captioned "Bavarian Alps near Berchtesgaden, Germany, 1933")

He wanted them
to call him "Onkle"
but these Bavarian kids—
    Sister in a dirndl
    Brother with a feather in his Alpine cap—
were troubled by his sharp nose,
his severely parted hair.
All the children were caught
in the camera's dark eye
half-dazed, open-mouthed
where his spirit must have crept in.
Each left his lap in tears,
ran to Mutti for comfort
who said "Habe keine Angst."*
But having taken the infection,
die Kinder knew better.

*Don't be afraid.

Shylock in Church*

Agnus Dei...
    Cold stones are hard on an old man's knees.
    I mime the words they force me to mouth.
    Up there, nailed to the Cross, their lord
    baring his breast,
    mooning over his great sacrifice,
    like the maudlin merchant before my knife.

Miserere Nobis...
    Please remember, ha shem, they came to "the Jew,"
    imploring gelt, I didn't seek them.
    One day they bow and call me "sir,"
    the next they stain my beard with rheum.
    If they knew mercy, they would have cut
    a pound of my flesh.

Ave Maria...
    Across the aisle my tokhter
    avoids my eyes, denies the bond.
    Big already with child, she sits with her goy.
    I am never to speak to die kinder, never to pass
    through their door, as if I were a stranger cur.
    And when the child grows older and asks,
    I will be long buried in my casket,
    a riddle that can't be unlocked.

Amen.

---

*In Shakespeare's "The Merchant of Venice," the life of Shylock, the Jewish moneylender, is spared on condition that he convert to Christianity.

Quasi-*

His face is cut into planes
      like a Cubist mask.
One cheek sags like a bladder,
      the other seems swollen in pain.
His eyes are mis-
      aligned. A bright one glares
at the Parisian mob, another,
      diffident, looks away.
Brother to the gargoyles
      that leer from the cathedral walls,
he is cursed with full awareness
      of his grotesque form.
When they whip him in the public square,
      does the dead flesh of his monstrous hump
feel the sting? Did Laughton,
      who was obese and gay,
wish that he too could be made of stone?

*Based on the 1939 film "The Hunchback of Notre Dame" starring Charles Laughton in the title role.

Hitchcock the Boy

He suspected there was always something
to atone for. Once, his father let the bobbies
lock him up; all night, he could hear
a flapping through the prison walls.
In the old tales Mother read to him when he was ill,
the harpies would peck out the eyes
of those who had trespassed.
At school, the other children used bright colors;
he preferred an inky sheen.
When the class recited the names of the monarchs,
he'd stare out the window that framed
the angular movements and sudden flights,
and at recess, when the others kicked a ball,
he observed the ominous way the crows gathered,
heard the menace in their call.

Chiller Theatre: The Bride

Just because he was lonely,
they arranged it without my consent.
I hissed at his goofy smile;
his intentions were quite plain:
he would jab it in like an animal
and it would be over just like that.
What girl in her right mind would prefer that oaf
to the handsome man at his side, the one
with the intelligent forehead.
He would know how a girl was made,
all her secret parts; only he knew
how to electrify her with a touch.

"Summer Interior" (1909)
Edward Hopper

We peer past a curtain
through a film of morning light.
She seems to have fallen,
an arm resting on the mattress,
the linens caught under her naked thigh.
The abrupt diagonal thrust of the unmade bed
slices through the frame.
Her face, cast down, burns scarlet,
scarlet is the coverlet, scarlet the stripes
on the blanket, scarlet bleeds into
the mahogany frame, stains the edges
of the creamy sheet, even
her swatch of dark pubic hair is cut
with a sliver of red.
How, then, can we gaze at her?
Why won't we look away?

Melville's Second Son*

They called me Stanny, never Stan,
though I was christened "Stanwix"
after the Fort great-grandfather defended
up in New York State.
After Barney put a bullet in his brain,
they didn't want to let me go.
Papa called me "fast fish."
The girls were gone much of the time:
Fannie with "that Philadelphia boy";
Bessie visiting cousins in western Mass.
But I was too near-sighted for dentistry
and Uncle's law firm held no allure.
Father had written about those South American ports
halfway to the tropics, with their veiled Spanish ladies
and corruption oozing from the white-washed walls.
Maybe I would find gold or I could raise sheep,
but even if I didn't, I would be climbing the mast,
chewing tobacco with the shirtless sailors,
learning to curse in Portuguese.
Barney had liked to pretend he was a soldier,
but I was the one who wanted to sail forbidden seas,
I was Ishmael, why couldn't Papa see?
He stamped on the hardwood floor, insisted I stay;
oh, he could play Ahab to the hilt.
But I baffled him with mildness.
"Father," I said,
"I would prefer not to."

---

*The author Herman Melville had four children: sons Malcolm (nicknamed Barney) and Stanwix, and daughters Elizabeth and Francis. Both sons pre-deceased him.

Forecast

Acorns slip through the leaves,
thud to the ground and bounce,
crusting the lawn with their broken caps
and tough fruit.
I crush them underfoot,
mow them into meal.
Still they fall. They ping
off the shingled roof,
frightening a flock of starlings
whose inky sheen screens the sun,
their reedy cry a song
of things to come.

Crossword

The day before,
tubed up to the machines,
Dad was still working those puzzles.
Still quick and sharp,
he peered through bi-focals
worn low down on his nose,
filling in the boxes
in his firm and flowing hand,
all those words still humming
through the circuits of his brain—
the synonyms and idioms,
the puns and proper names.
His fingers still retained
their tensile strength—
bold, clear letters never straying
outside the grid.

But he couldn't beat that puzzle
underneath the flesh—
the clues indecipherable,
the answers obscure, the dark spaces
tightening and closing in.

The Immigrants
(9/11/2002)

As they descended over the bay
on that glittering Tuesday morning,
the sun lit the east side of the city—
Chinatown, little Italy, Hester Street.
Almost all of them could claim connection
to one part of its grid. An ancestor
had come through its port, there,
down below, near the copper statue
that even now they had to gawk at.
To be entering the golden land,
to see the towers loom
at impossible heights—
this was the immigrant's dream
gone bad. They must have
gripped the armrests,
thought of loved ones left
on another shore, and awaited the shock
of this new world.

Between Two Houses

I probably won't die in Brooklyn
  my father died in Brooklyn
    my mother will probably die in Brooklyn
      or maybe a hospital in the city
But I probably won't.
It'll be down south in this valley
  between the slate blue hills
    if it's spring the dogwood blossoms
      will be open pink and white
But only briefly.

I remember spring in Brooklyn
  I remember the closed-in alley
    my father's easy toss
      the bubble-gum pink Spaldeen
slapping my palm.
I remember the sound
  echoing in the narrow passage
    between the two houses
      my mother's dinner call ending the game
I probably won't die here.

White Out

The striated cap puts up
a crusty resistance.
Though the gluey fluid
has all but dried up,
its chemical smell is instantly released
like a genie from the lamp.

My wish is to undo
with a few swift strokes,
to paint over the errors,
erase the uncongenial phrase,
mute the careless, hurtful words,
the way fallen snow
muffles the harsh sounds of the world;
and then, from that clean, winter landscape
to bring forth
the words meant to stay.

Infinitive

When a nurse told us they had cleaned you up,
we entered carefully, unsure of how to approach
you in your mystery.
Wasn't there supposed to be
a way to talk to the dead,
a template even for this?

You did not resemble sleep.
No dreams danced beneath your eyelids.
Your body was already cool to the touch,
abstract, like a stillborn verb:
uninflected, without tense, mood
or person.

Objects in Mirror

Mom and Dad, for example,
who appear to be cloudy and distant;
or the assigned seat of that girl—
Judy Heller—in 7th grade,
vacant the rest of that year;
or Gary's gas-guzzling Chevy—
battered grille, shattered glass—
forgotten until April
like the forsythia's blinding spears.
There's some kind of trick lens
inside us, pushing everything back
until they seem to disappear.
You must stay alert: these objects
are much closer than they appear.

In the event that…

Imagine an ailment which robbed you
of humor, dulled your sharp relish
for the absurd—your eye blind
to the incongruous, your ear deaf
to irony, your blood stream sluggish
from lack of wit. Imagine suffering
such a debilitating disease.
      …I would say, please
      do not resuscitate, please
      remove from all life support.

A King of Tweets and Twitters
(November 9, 2016)

Look here on this portrait
of an elegant, honorable man
whose unruffled brow bespeaks a nobility of mind.
Here is a grace that gave the world assurance
of his charitable intents.
Look you now upon this counterfeit likeness
of a bloated braggart, a blot upon nature,
exuding a lurid amber light
whose rich garments belie the poverty of his soul.
How is it you could step
from this to this?
Have you eyes? Have you judgment?
Sure your wits are atrophied or else
you could not turn from a sage to a satyr,
from a mensch to a mountebank.
Such an act beggars the imagination
and makes fools of all our prophets.
Frailty, thy name is voter.

So Many Things

When I retire, there are so many things
I don't want to do:

I won't write my memoirs
or sail to exotic ports.

Please don't ask me to ballroom dance.

I shalt not:
        Sky dive
        Climb a Mountain
        Run a marathon.

You won't catch me checking your name at the polls
or welcoming you to Wal-Mart.
I won't be that old guy who bags your groceries
or delivers the newspaper at 5 a.m.

I don't want to fill my time,
I want to empty it,

gliding my bike along the Riverway,
taking in the so many things I missed
in my haste.

The Recliner

To lie supine
  floating in space
or to sit upright
  feet planted on the ground,
that is the question.
Shall I be vigilant
  or laid-back,
on guard or at ease
  or somewhere in-between?

With a press of a button,
  I begin to rise:
knees unbend, head tilts back,
  I seem to be suspended in a bubble.
What luxury to lie prone,
  to have this Schubert adagio
wash over me, to be unburdened
  of choice…
But now my Hamlet-mind turns to
  the satisfactions of this solid earth:
to be grounded by gravity,
  able to tap out the furious beat
of the scherzo, feel the full percussive force
  of the hardwood floor
tingle the balls of my toes.
      Seeking that middle way
  between extremes,
I press reverse and hold,
  trying to locate
the g-spot of recliner bliss:
     There…that's it…no…
     maybe one more click…wait..
     there it is, ah…

Have I attained the Goldilocks ideal at last
or am I doomed forever to over-correct,
restlessly shifting between safe and sorry,
too little and too much?

Introduction to Italian

The world seems an agreeable place this semester,
    Un posto piacevole,
and my fellow humans, *le umanita,*
gracious and kind—*molto gentile.*
Everything rhymes in Italian, everything chimes:
    Ronzoni sono buoni.
When my 30-something children visit,
all weekend I address them as *i miei bambini*
and we gesture dramatically and hug each other
as if the language has warmed our blood.

This morning, I listen to a guitar quintet
by Luigi Boccherrini, bewitched by the graceful *cantabile,*
moved deeply by the *pastorale.*
And later, when I enter the garage,
    my rusty old Schwinn has been transformed into
        Una bicicletta classica.
    Gliding it along the New on this crisp autumn day,
    even the birds seem to be singing,
        Fe-li-ce, Fe-li-ce, Fe-li-ce.

Baffled*

His tiny claws scrabble
on the slick surface of the metal dome.
He scratches furiously at the thing,
fighting the helpless slide down,
then somehow manages to re-gain his perch.
He puffs his cheeks out, his tail quivers.
Baffled by the uncanny disc,
he eyes the feeder from a nearby limb.

Now is not the time for doubt or apprehension;
no dwelling on your lost opportunities.
You always took your due portion for granted.
Now you'll have to exercise your wit
to get at the prize, improvise a way,
trust in your prehensile grip
to keep you attached.
Go ahead, fling yourself across the gap,
hang upside down, inch your way forward, stretch yourself
in ways you didn't think possible.

*Certain bird feeders, specifically designed to prevent squirrels from eating the seed, are known as "baffles."

In My Dotage

Reading the Stoics with my coffee,
seeking wisdom in my dotage.
Marcus Aurelius counsels patience:
"Nothing is endless," he says.
Has he been to the DMV?

Epictetus cautions us to keep our cool:
"To be enraged is not manly."
Yet my blood simmers daily;
how does one maintain composure
in the age of Trump?

Seneca believes servitude is self-imposed;
we're all enslaved by old habits,
daily routines, tethered by cables
to our inescapable machines.

"Philosophy is the art of confronting death,"
my professor pronounced on the first day of class.
        (He stole that from Cicero).
I wasn't 18, thought this profound
and typed a long essay, in 1 sitting,
on the existential epistemology of Fyodor Dostoyevsky
after smoking some good weed.

Now, I'm nearing 70 (how terribly strange)
and Cato the Younger tells me I mustn't kvetch,
"Amor Fati," embrace your fate,
learn to acquiesce. So, like Camus,
I try to imagine Sisyphus happy…
>   There he is in the pit,
>   rocking and rolling, bearing the weight,
>   feeling the gritty sandstone
>   bite into his palms.
>   He breathes evenly, shifting his center of gravity
>   as he slowly climbs.
>   Each time he falls back, he pauses,
>   considers a new strategy to minimize the pain,
>   adjusts his stance so as to maintain a fine balance
>   between hope and despair.

Jeff Saperstein was born and raised in Brooklyn, New York (long before it became "cool"). After living in New England for a decade, in 1985 he and his wife moved to the unlikely little town of Radford in the beautiful New River Valley of southwestern Virginia, where they have lived ever since. A Yankee in Appalachia, Jeff is often amused and inspired by his curious geographic journey.

Jeff's poems have appeared in numerous literary magazines, including *Main Street Rag*, *The Sow's Ear*, *The Deronda Review*, *Still Crazy*, *Ibbetson Street Press*, *The Stickman Review*, and *Floyd County Moonshine*. He was the featured poet in the September 2012 issue of *Chantarelle's Notebook*. His poem, "The Minimalist," won first prize in the annual *Common Ground Review* poetry contest in 2011.

Since retiring from teaching English at Radford University in 2015, Jeff enjoys bike riding along the New River, listening to classical music very early in the morning, bird watching, and hanging out with his two dogs and one cat. He and his wife Lisa have two adult children, Jacob and Jennie.

Jeff can be contacted at jsaperstein1623@gmail.com

www.ingramcontent.com/pod-product-compliance
Lightning Source LLC
LaVergne TN
LVHW041504070426
835507LV00012B/1313